# TALK ABOUT
# Sex and Puberty

**Sarah Levete**

WAYLAND

First published in 2009 by Wayland

Copyright © Wayland 2009

Wayland
338 Euston Road
London NW1 3BH

Wayland Australia
Level 17/207 Kent Street
Sydney, NSW 2000

Produced for Wayland by Calcium

Editors: Sarah Eason and Robyn Hardyman
Editor for Wayland: Katie Powell
Consultant: Jayne Wright
Designers: Paul Myerscough and Rob Norridge
Picture researcher: Maria Joannou

British Library Cataloguing in Publication Data:
Levete, Sarah.
    Talk about sex and puberty.
    1. Sex (Biology)—Juvenile literature. 2. Puberty—Juvenile
    literature. 3. Adolescence—Juvenile literature.
    I. Title II. Sex and puberty
    612.6-dc22

ISBN: 978 0 7502 5738 1

Printed in Malaysia

Wayland is a division of Hachette Children's Books, an Hachette UK Company
www.hachette.co.uk

The majority of situations in this publication are fictitious and are posed by models.
Any resemblance to real persons, living or dead, is purely coincidental.

The website addresses (URLs) included in this book were valid at the time of going to press.
However, because of the nature of the Internet, it is possible that some addresses may have
changed, or sites may have changed or closed down since publication. While the author and
Publisher regret any inconvenience this may cause the readers, no responsibility for any
such changes can be accepted by either the author or the Publisher.

Every attempt has been made to clear copyright. Should there be any inadvertent omission
please apply to the publisher for rectification.

The author and publisher would like to thank the following for allowing their pictures
to be reproduced in this publication:
Cover photograph: Alamy Images: Susan Vogel.
Interior photographs: Alamy Images: Susan Vogel 8, Corbis: Tim Pannell 19; Dreamstime:
Barsik 36; Fotolia: Marie C 28; Istockphoto: Asiseeit 40, Digitalskillet 41, Eileen Hart 38–39,
Alain Juteau 35, Michael Krinke 7, Renee Lee 20, Dawn Liljenquist 42, Aldo Murillo 13, Alex
Nikada 16, Chris Schmidt 10, 26, Reuben Schulz 45; Photolibrary: Glamour International 11;
Rex Features: Sipa Press 21; Science Photo Library: D. Phillips 23, Mark Thomas 30–31;
Shutterstock: Oguz Aral 18, Galina Barskaya 5, 14, Diego Cervo 33, Charbnica 12, Mandy
Godbehear 4, Mika Heittola 29, Iofoto 17, MalibuBooks 22, Monkey Business Images 6, 24–25,
27, 32, 37, Aleynikov Pavel 43, Ronen 34, Dmitriy Shironosov 1, Juliya W. Shumskaya 15,
Ronald Sumners 9; Wayland Archive: 47.

# CONTENTS

# Chapter 1

# What is puberty?

**O**ne day you look at yourself in the mirror and notice that you look a bit different – perhaps there is new hair growing on parts of your body, or your body shape is changing. Don't panic, everyone goes through this process of change and development, which is called puberty. As you change from a child into a young adult, your body matures and your emotions develop. These changes prepare you for adulthood.

## Preparing for adulthood

Puberty doesn't just make you look and act more grown-up. It also prepares the body for reproduction, which is having children. However, being physically capable of having sex and reproducing does not mean that a person is emotionally ready for sexual relationships and possible parenthood. Physical maturity can happen long before a person is emotionally ready to deal with sexual relationships and sexual maturity.

*It is reassuring to have friends who are also going through puberty and experiencing similar changes.*

There is another period of change and development that often overlaps with puberty, and this is called adolescence. This refers more to the social and emotional development of young people as they leave childhood and enter adulthood. Teenagers are often called adolescents.

## It happens to everyone

Puberty can be a confusing time. During puberty, people often have anxieties about how they are changing – it's common to wonder if you are normal. Rest assured, you are. Don't worry, puberty isn't physically painful.

Puberty is just the beginning of a long and exciting journey towards adulthood. This journey is made much easier if you understand the changes that take place during puberty and how they might affect your life. You can reassure yourself that everything is alright by asking questions, reading books like this one, and checking out some recommended websites on the Internet (see page 47).

*You may go through quite a few emotional ups and downs during puberty.*

Puberty doesn't change who you are; it simply enables you to mature physically and emotionally. After puberty, you'll look older, you'll be a slightly different shape, and you'll experience new feelings – but you will still be the same person as you were before puberty.

# It happened to me

'I went to the park with some friends and was wearing my usual sort of T-shirt. A couple of boys started to snigger and giggle. I suddenly realized they were laughing at me – just because my breasts were showing. Part of me wanted to curl up in a corner and hide but another part of me felt proud – I was growing up.'

Ellie, aged 11.

## When does puberty start?

Girls usually start puberty earlier than boys, around the age of 11, but it can start any time between the ages of eight and 13. For boys, puberty usually starts around the age of 12, but it can be any time between the ages of nine and 15. If you are worried that you have started puberty much earlier or later than these ages, ask your parents or carers to arrange for a check-up with your doctor, just to reassure you.

You might feel embarrassed and a bit left out if you are more advanced than your friends, or if you haven't yet started puberty and they have. There are plenty of people in a similar situation. If you are ahead of your friends, they may be longing to ask you questions. On the other hand, if a good friend has started puberty before you, use the opportunity to ask them some questions.

The age at which puberty starts is largely decided by your genes. These are the building blocks of a person's physical make-up and are inherited from parents and grandparents. However, in some more economically developed countries there is evidence that puberty can begin earlier – at about age seven for some girls. Possible causes include eating more foods with artificial chemicals, which copy the actions of the puberty-stimulating chemicals in the body, and being overweight and inactive.

*Physical changes, such as your breasts growing, are a sign that you are going through puberty and that you are growing up.*

# TALK ABOUT

✱ **Have you experienced any of the changes that occur during puberty?**

✱ **Why do you think it is useful to be aware of the facts and issues about puberty and sex?**

# How does puberty start?

You can't tell your body when to start and stop puberty – it's out of your control. Puberty doesn't happen overnight, it usually lasts for several years.

Without you feeling or knowing anything about it, puberty starts in a part of the brain called the hypothalamus. The hypothalamus sends chemicals called hormones to the pituitary gland at the base of the brain. This stimulates the pituitary gland to send other hormones around the body. Hormones are natural chemicals which travel around the body in the blood, instructing parts of the body to develop and behave in particular ways.

Hormones kick-start the physical changes of puberty. Both boys' and girls' bodies release hormones, but their effects are different as they work on different parts of the body. In girls, hormones stimulate the ovaries to produce sex hormones called oestrogen and progesterone. In boys, hormones stimulate the testes to produce the sex hormone testosterone.

*Testosterone is the hormone responsible for building muscle in boys as they go through puberty.*

The release of these sex hormones triggers the development of the sex or reproductive organs. Sex organs on the outside of the body are also called genitals. This is the vulva for girls and the penis for boys. Sex hormones also trigger other changes such as the growth of breasts or facial hair. All these changes are explained in this book.

## Signs of puberty

During puberty, people usually have a growth spurt and grow several centimetres in one year. Girls are often taller than boys at this stage, simply because they start puberty earlier.

You will notice hair starting to grow around your genitals. This is called pubic hair because it grows around the pubes, the area of the body just below the abdomen. It can be a different colour from the hair on your head. The hair is usually soft at first, but it becomes coarser and thicker over time.

Hair also begins to grow more thickly elsewhere on the body, such as the legs and underarms. Boys may notice hair growth on their backs and chests, and faces (see pages 16–17). Some girls eventually decide to shave, use creams or wax to remove underarm and leg hair, but this must be done carefully.

Changing hormone levels make you sweat more and smell different. Sweat isn't smelly in itself, but it can begin to smell when it mixes with the bacteria on the skin. Regular washing and using deodorant helps to make sure you smell fresh.

*Boys often begin to grow facial hair during puberty. Many choose to shave it.*

## Spots

Hormones are also responsible for spots, a common and unwelcome feature of puberty. Glands in the skin called sebaceous glands release more of an oily substance called sebum. If this builds up, the sebaceous glands can become infected and a red spot or a whitehead or blackhead forms. Spots can break out on the face and neck, and the shoulders and back. Acne is a large outbreak of spots. Doctors can prescribe creams to help reduce severe acne. Spots are a fact of life for everyone. Doctors and chemists are used to giving adults and teenagers advice or help in dealing with spots – there's no need to be embarrassed.

The extra sebum that is produced in the skin during puberty often makes your hair look and feel greasy, too.

*Try to resist the temptation to pick spots – it will only make them worse and more noticeable.*

# DOs & DON'Ts

**During puberty, keeping clean and being fit both help to keep some of the less welcome effects of hormonal change under control.**

* Do wash regularly with soap and use a deodorant or antiperspirant.

* Don't pick spots – they will spread. Put some antiseptic cream on them. Don't be embarrassed – everyone has spots at some point.

* Do keep your skin clean and keep your hair back from your face, to stop your face becoming greasier.

* Do drink plenty of water – this helps keep the skin fresh.

* Do take some exercise to keep you feeling fit.

* Don't eat junk foods – a healthy balanced diet which includes plenty of fruit and vegetables can help to minimize spotty outbreaks.

* Don't feel alone: puberty happens to everyone.

# Chapter 2

# What happens to girls during puberty?

**G**irls' bodies change shape quite noticeably during puberty. They put on some weight. This isn't down to bad diet, it's nature's way of making the body more womanly so that it is prepared for pregnancy and giving birth. The hips and bottom usually get curvier – this is a sign of growing up, not of being fat. It's not a good idea to go on a slimming diet at this time – it's much better to eat a healthy, balanced diet and to exercise regularly.

## Breasts

Growing breasts is one of a girl's first signs of puberty. Breasts begin as small swellings or lumps under the nipples. As breasts grow, the area around them may feel a bit sensitive or sore. It's quite usual for one breast to be larger or smaller than the other – in time this evens out, but no woman's breasts are exactly the same.

Girls often worry about their breast size or shape, but everyone has different shaped and sized breasts – and one shape or size is no better than another. If your breasts begin to grow before your friends', you may feel a bit self-conscious, especially during swimming lessons or PE. But your friends may well be feeling a bit envious that they don't have breasts yet. Everyone develops at a different rate – you'll all have breasts eventually.

*If you look at yourself and your friends, you will see that you all are a different shape and size. This is quite normal.*

*Try to choose a bra that fits properly and feels comfortable.*

## Wearing a bra

Many girls and women feel more comfortable wearing a bra to support their breasts. It's important that your bra fits properly. In some shops an assistant can measure you to make sure you get the right size.

Measure your breasts regularly and buy new bras as they grow. The size and shape of your breasts will change throughout your life, so have regular bra fittings.

# FACTS

Bra sizes are given in letters and numbers. The letters refer to the cup size – the rounded part of the breast that fits in a bra's 'cup'. The numbers refer to the chest measurement.

To measure yourself for a bra, use a soft tape measure and ask your mum or a good friend to help.

Chest size: measure just under the breasts and around the back. If the measurement is an even number add 10 centimetres (cm) or 4 inches; if it is an odd number add 12.5 cm or 5 inches.

Cup size: measure from the fullest part of the breasts around the back. Subtract the chest size from this measurement and then use this chart.

1 in (2.5 cm) smaller = cup AA

Same cup and chest size = A

1 in (2.5 cm) larger = B

2 in (5 cm) larger = C

3 in (7.5 cm) larger = D

4 in (10 cm) larger = DD

5 in (12.5 cm) larger = E

6 in (15 cm) larger = F

7 in (17.5 cm) larger = G

8 in (20 cm) larger = H

## Sex organs

Puberty prepares the body to reproduce. In girls, the reproductive or sex organs develop in readiness to conceive and grow a baby. Many of these changes take place inside the body, but some also take place outside it, such as growing breasts to produce milk to feed a baby.

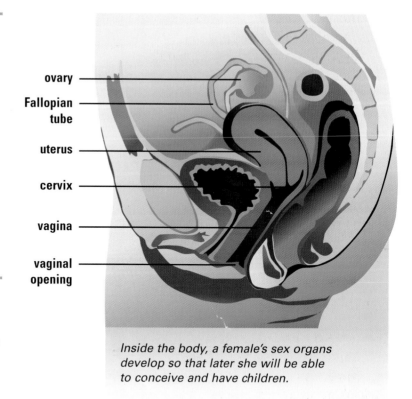

ovary
Fallopian tube
uterus
cervix
vagina
vaginal opening

*Inside the body, a female's sex organs develop so that later she will be able to conceive and have children.*

## Keeping clean

The vagina produces fluids to keep it moist and clean. This discharge may produce whitish stains on your underwear, which is quite normal. Keep your vagina clean by washing regularly. If the discharge becomes smelly, you may have an infection called thrush. Your doctor can prescribe antibiotics to clear up it up. Anyone can get thrush, and it doesn't mean you are not keeping yourself clean.

## Female internal organs

### Ovaries
The two ovaries are organs in the lower abdomen. They make the eggs, called ova, which are the sex cells. At birth, a baby girl is born with all the eggs she will use during her adult life, but they remain undeveloped until puberty. Then, the hormones stimulate an egg to ripen.

### Fallopian tubes
These narrow tubes connect the ovaries to the uterus, or womb. A ripened egg passes along one of them towards the uterus. If a sperm meets the egg here, it fertilizes it and an embryo develops.

### Uterus

The uterus, or womb, is a pear-shaped organ. A fertilized egg implants in the wall of the uterus, which stretches during pregnancy to make space for a growing baby.

### Cervix

This is the opening at the base of the uterus.

### Vagina

The vaginal canal is a muscular tube that leads from the cervix to the outside of the body. It can contract (get smaller) or expand (get larger). The penis fits into the vagina during sex; blood from the uterus passes through the vagina during menstruation. This is called a period. During birth, a baby passes out of the vagina.

*During pregnancy, a woman's uterus expands to allow the baby inside to grow and develop.*

## Female external organs

The female genitals on the outside of the body are called the vulva. You can see your vulva by looking in a mirror. Everyone's looks slightly different. The vulva covers the opening to the vagina. It is made up of:

### Labia

The labia are flaps of skin that cover the vagina's opening. The outer labia have pubic hair on them. They cover the inner labia, which do not have hair.

### Clitoris

The clitoris is a small pea-sized organ, which is very sensitive to touch. It is at the front of the vulva, where the labia join. There is a fold of skin over the clitoris.

### Vaginal opening

The vaginal opening leads to the vagina.

## That time of the month

For girls, puberty means the beginning of menstruation, or periods. These continue through all the years when a woman is capable of having children, except during pregnancy. They finish at the time called the menopause, when a woman stops producing eggs and is no longer able to have children. The menopause usually begins when a woman is about 50.

An ovary releases an egg into the Fallopian tube – this is called ovulation. Meanwhile, the lining of the uterus has been thickening in preparation to house a fertilized egg. If the egg is not fertilized, it falls apart and leaves the body along with the uterus's thicker lining. This is the reddish flow that leaves the vagina during a period. This menstrual flow is made up of a small amount of blood from blood vessels that break away from the uterus wall, cells from the uterus lining and sticky fluid from the cervix.

*A period can sometimes give you stomach cramps but they can be relieved during exercise.*

## Dates

On average, periods run on a 28-day cycle, and often last between three and five days. Use a notebook or diary to keep a record of when your period starts and how long it lasts. You may begin to see a regular pattern to your cycle, although some women always have irregular periods. It helps to know roughly when your periods are due once you have begun to have sexual relationships – missing a period is the first sign of pregnancy.

## Keeping fresh

There are several ways to cope with your period. You can use sanitary pads or towels in your knickers to soak up the menstrual flow. Change them every few hours, and first thing in the morning, so that you do not 'leak' or become smelly. Tampons can be inserted into the vagina – they soak up the blood from the inside. It's very important to change a tampon every four to eight hours to avoid infection.

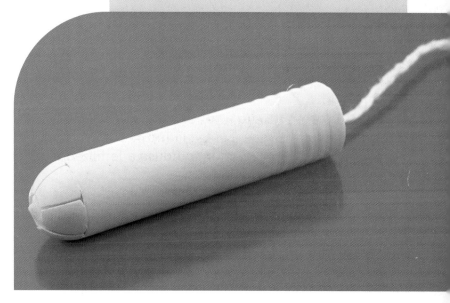

When you use a tampon, gently push it inside your vagina and leave the string hanging down. After a few hours or when you need a fresh tampon, use the string to pull it out.

# DOs & DON'Ts

✻ **Don't be embarrassed – every girl and woman has periods.**

✻ **Do change sanitary towels and tampons regularly.**

✻ **Don't throw sanitary pads down the toilet – they'll block it up.**

✻ **Do put sanitary pads in a special bin, or in a bag and then in the waste bin. It is best to do this with tampons, too.**

✻ **Do carry a spare sanitary pad or tampon in your bag, just in case.**

✻ **Do cuddle up to a hot-water bottle if you have period pains such as back or stomach ache. The discomfort is caused as the uterus wall contracts to get rid of its thicker lining.**

✻ **Don't avoid exercise when you have a period – with sanitary pads or tampons you can do most activities (except swimming if using pads). Gentle exercise can help with period pains, too.**

# Chapter 3

# What happens to boys during puberty?

**F**rom a deepening voice to a hairy chin, there are lots of obvious signs that a boy is going through puberty. If you feel self-conscious about your appearance, just remember that it happens to everyone.

## The voice breaks

A young boy's voice is softer and higher than an adult male's. Puberty changes that, 'breaking' the voice. This is when the larynx, or voice box, gets bigger and makes the voice sound deeper. Sometimes the change takes a while – and during this time the voice can sound a bit squeaky. It's quite normal, although it may feel a bit embarrassing. Choirboys who have very pure, high voices haven't yet started puberty. Once their voices break, they won't be able to reach such high notes.

*Regular exercise keeps you fit and helps make you feel good about your changing body shape.*

## Changing shape

The hormone testosterone starts to race around a boy's body during puberty. As well as instructing the sex organs to develop, it makes muscles grow, especially around the arms and shoulders. You may not feel any stronger, but you will probably look it! If you don't have any muscles yet, don't worry. All the changes in puberty take a long time to complete. Eating a healthy, balanced diet and taking regular exercise will help you to make the most of your body shape – you can't change it but you can keep your body fit.

You may be worried that you are growing breasts if you notice small fleshy swellings under your nipples. But you aren't growing breasts like a girl – it's just a natural growth and they will disappear.

## Hair

As well as the hair that grows on the rest of your body, one of the first signs of puberty in boys is the appearance of facial hair. At first it can look a bit fluffy and patchy, starting with a light moustache. When the hair is thick enough, some boys decide to shave it (using an electric shaver or a razor with foamy soap and water); others decide to grow a beard.

*If you are finding puberty difficult, it might help to talk to a friend who is going through the same changes, too.*

# DOs & DON'Ts

✳ **Don't shave until there is enough stubble to get rid of – otherwise the skin becomes sore.**

✳ **Do shave in front of a mirror otherwise you'll cut your skin. If this happens, wash the cut in cold water then put a bit of tissue over it.**

✳ **Do shave in the direction in which the hair grows.**

✳ **Do dab your skin with moisturizer or aftershave to soothe it after shaving.**

✳ **Don't shave over moles – it's safer to trim the hairs with scissors.**

# Sex organs

The appearance of a boy's sex organs changes early in puberty, in order to be able to reproduce. A boy's penis and testicles grow in preparation for sexual intercourse and the fertilization of an egg.

*Testicles*
The two testicles, often called balls, get bigger and start to produce sperm.

penis

glans

testicle

scrotum

One of the first outward signs of puberty for boys is the development of their sex organs.

*Scrotum*
The scrotum is a wrinkly bag of skin which holds the testicles. At puberty, the skin of the scrotum becomes redder. The scrotum keeps the testicles at the right temperature to produce sperm. If the body gets cold, the scrotum shrinks; if it gets too hot, the scrotum becomes larger and floppier.

*Penis*
During puberty, hair grows around the base of the penis. The penis is usually soft. The main part of it is called the shaft.

*Glans*
The tip of the penis is called the glans, or head. Semen and urine pass out of the penis through an opening at the top of the glans.

*Foreskin*
The foreskin covers the top of the penis. Some cultures and religious faiths remove the foreskin, and sometimes it is removed for health reasons. This is called circumcision. If you have a foreskin, wash gently under it regularly.

## Erections

Boys often have erections – this is when the penis becomes larger and stiffens, sticking away from the body. When a male is sexually excited, more blood flows into the penis. The purpose of this is so that the penis can fit into the vagina and sperm can swim up the vagina to fertilize the egg.

Stimulation of an erection often results in ejaculation. A whitish fluid called semen spurts out of the penis – semen contains sperm. The testicles make 1,000 sperm per second! Any sperm that are not released through ejaculation are absorbed back into the body.

During puberty, you may wake up and notice that the sheets or your pyjamas are damp. This is caused by a 'wet' dream – you might be dreaming about something sexy that makes you ejaculate in your sleep. It's nothing to be ashamed of. Most boys have wet dreams at this time. If you don't want to tell anyone, put your pyjamas in the washing machine and get a clean pair, or wear pants in bed.

*Boys often worry about the size of their penises, but remember that it is perfectly normal for penises to come in many shapes and sizes.*

# DOs & DON'Ts

✱ Don't worry about the size of your penis – there is no right or wrong size.

✱ Sometimes an erection happens for no reason – try not to feel embarrassed. Think of something boring, like homework, and it might go away.

✱ Do wash your penis and scrotum regularly.

# Chapter 4

# What are sexual feelings?

The physical changes of puberty make a person more aware of their sexual parts while the release of hormones activates sexual feelings, such as fancying someone and having sexual thoughts. The primary function of sex is to reproduce. For a couple who are both mature enough emotionally and physically, sex is also a way of expressing love and affection.

## Is it just about sex?

During puberty, many young people begin to discover and explore their own sex parts, touching and enjoying them. This is called masturbation. As long as this experimentation takes place in private, there is nothing wrong with this and it is nothing to be ashamed of.

Sexual feelings may result in a couple kissing, hugging and touching. Sharing and enjoying sexual feelings doesn't have to lead to sexual intercourse. Sexual activity is very intimate, and should only be done in private.

*During puberty, many young people begin to feel attracted to other people.*

*There is lots of emphasis in the media on looking sexy, but remember that having sex doesn't make a person grown-up or cool.*

# In the media

Society today is very sexualized. We are bombarded with images of sex. On advertising billboards, in film, on TV, in magazines, sex is everywhere, from couples stroking each other to nearly naked women or men draped over cars or perfumes. It can seem as if having some sort of sexual relationship or feelings is a mark of being grown-up and cool. It isn't. Sex is only one aspect of adult life. It can be a very positive experience when a person is emotionally ready, and only then.

## Be informed

At school, there is probably a lot of rumour, whispering and giggling about sex. Some people find it very embarrassing to talk about. Others think that talking about it makes them seem older and more grown-up.

If a friend tells you something about sex, he or she may not have got it completely right. It's best to check out the facts in books or talk to an adult you trust if you have questions. You could ask your parents, but if that is too embarrassing ask an older sibling or another relative you trust. Schools offer sex education and relationship advice in the curriculum, so you can ask your teacher. The question you ask is probably the one that everyone else is longing to ask. The more informed you are about the facts, the easier it is to make safe decisions.

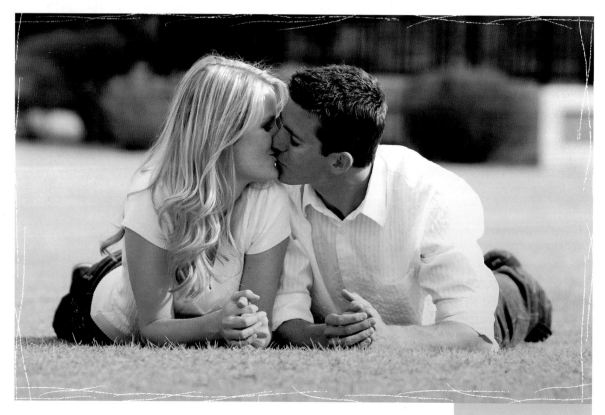

## What happens during sex?

Sexual intercourse is when a male puts his erect penis into a female's vagina. He reaches a climax, or peak of excitement, and ejaculates: semen, containing sperm, spurts out of the penis. Sperm swim up the vagina to the Fallopian tubes, where one sperm may fertilize an egg if one is present. That's the biological bit, but there's a lot more to it than that.

*Sex is a physical act, but it is also about showing love and affection to your partner.*

# DOs & DON'Ts

✳ **Don't feel pressurized into any kind of sexual activity, whether it's kissing or intercourse.**

✳ **Do tell an adult you trust if you have anxieties about a sexual relationship.**

✳ **Don't be ashamed of sexual feelings – they are a natural part of growing up and are to be enjoyed, as long as they don't harm anyone else.**

Touching the lips, breasts or sex parts can excite or arouse someone. These pleasurable sexual feelings can make a person's body feel tingly. Most couples cuddle, kiss, stroke and touch each other before having sex. This is called foreplay and prepares the body for sex. A woman's body releases a fluid in the vagina to make it easier for the erect penis to enter.

During sex, the man and woman move around so that the penis moves in and out or around the vagina. This increases the pleasure. The couple may also masturbate or touch each other as well. Often both women and men 'come', or feel an intense pleasure called an orgasm. When this happens to the man, he ejaculates.

Once young people reach the age of consent, it doesn't mean they ought to be having sex. Deciding to have sex is a very personal decision, and it is important that people wait until they really feel ready.

# FACTS

The age at which a person can legally have sex is called the age of consent. This is when they are considered mature enough to consent (agree) to and understand the implications of a sexual relationship. The age of consent is different in different countries.

Age of consent between members of the opposite sex:

* Germany: 14 unless the older partner is over 18 and considered to be taking advantage of the younger partner.

* United Kingdom: 16. (Northern Ireland: 17).

* United States: varies in different states but generally between 16 and 18.

* Mexico: 12.

It is illegal to have sex with someone who is under age.

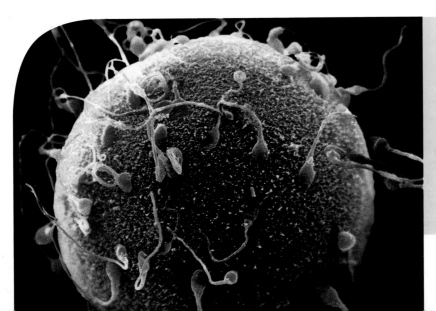

When a man ejaculates during sex, millions of sperm swim up the vagina to the Fallopian tube. There they meet the woman's egg, as shown in this magnified image. Usually, only one sperm will fuse and fertilize the egg.

## When is the right time to start having sex?

A person's body may be physically mature enough to have sex and have children, but that doesn't mean that the person is emotionally ready. Before starting any sexual relationship, there are lots things to consider.

Sex will become an important part of most couple's relationships. It is an expression of love and affection between two people. You are much more likely to feel good, safe and confident about sex if you have made a considered decision about when and with whom to first have it. Be aware also about laws regarding the age of consent (page 23).

## Sex and marriage

Some people decide not to have sex until they marry. They want to keep a sexual relationship special and unique to the person who they fall in love with, and with whom they want to spend the rest of their lives. Other people wait until they feel ready to commit to a particular relationship.

# DOs & DON'Ts

✳ Don't feel pressurized into starting a sexual relationship.

✳ Don't start a sexual relationship just because your friends are having sex.

✳ Do make sure you feel safe and comfortable with your partner before starting a sexual relationship.

## Changing views about sex

Sixty years ago, sex was a taboo subject – it was not really discussed openly. Today, however, people recognize the importance of being properly informed about sex. Understanding the issues involved can help people make choices about when to start a sexual relationship, and to avoid unwanted pregnancies and sexually transmitted infections (STIs – see pages 28–31).

Some parents and families have strong views on whether or not a young person should be allowed to have sex. Some young people follow the advice and views of their parents and others do not. Some religions express strong views about sexual relationships; for instance, Christianity and Islam do not agree with sex outside marriage.

## Be aware

Many young people experiment with drinking alcohol. It's important to be aware of the risks of this, relating to sex. Drinking alcohol makes people feel relaxed and feel more confident. The effect of alcohol on the brain distorts thinking; it can affect a person's judgement about whether or not to have sex. Being drunk can affect a person's ability to clearly say no to sex, or to make sure they use contraception.

*Don't feel pressurized into having sex by your friends or peers. Wait until it feels right for you.*

# TALK ABOUT

* Do you think that having sex means you are grown-up?
* Do you think that choosing not to have sex is a sign of weakness or strength?
* How do you think a person knows when he or she is ready for a sexual relationship?

## What's all the fuss about?

Sex is not always what it's cracked up to be, especially at first. There are plenty of glamorous images of film stars looking beautiful and relaxed as they enjoy a sexual relationship – the reality is often different. At first, many people find sexual relationships awkward and not as pleasurable as they expected. This is quite usual and, like anything, it takes time to find confidence in sex. Having a trusting and caring partner makes it easier to feel safe and to develop confidence and enjoyment.

## Overwhelming feelings

During puberty, with the awakening of sexual feelings, it's very common for young people to have a crush on someone, often someone a bit older. It may be a teacher or someone in a position of authority. Crushes can make you think about the person the whole time. The person may be someone of the same sex or the opposite sex, someone you know or someone famous. Crushes are safe ways of having sexual and strong emotional feelings without becoming sexually active. If you are worried about your feelings, talk to someone you trust.

*Puberty can be a confusing time and some young people may think they are in love with an older person, such as a teacher. These feelings are probably just a crush.*

## Questions about sexuality

During puberty, as a person becomes aware of his or her sexual feelings, he or she may also begin to wonder about his or her sexuality. This is whether or not a person is sexually attracted to people of the opposite sex, the same sex or both sexes. The physical and emotional changes of puberty raise many questions about one's sexuality; there is often no clear immediate answer.

A heterosexual person is sexually attracted to people of the opposite sex. A homosexual person is sexually attracted to someone of the same sex. Homosexuality is also known as being gay. A woman attracted to a woman is also called a lesbian. A person who is bisexual is attracted to members of both sexes. In the past, being homosexual was considered to be wrong. Today, many people around the world are openly gay and are respected just like anyone else. Sexuality is just the way a person is.

*Instead of trying to define your sexuality, focus on enjoying all your friendships.*

Many people going through puberty feel attracted to members of their own sex. This doesn't necessarily mean they are homosexual, and it doesn't necessarily mean they are not. It can take several years to feel confident about your sexuality.

# It happened to me

'All my friends liked girls at school. But I wasn't really that interested. I felt a strong attraction to this other boy. Did that mean I was gay, or did it mean I just had a crush? I was really confused, frightened and embarrassed about my feelings. I plucked up my courage and confided in an older cousin who was really cool about it. He said he had felt the same when he was my age and lots of people are unsure about their feelings. So, for the moment, I'm just enjoying being with my friends and having a good time.'

Eddie, aged 15.

# Chapter 5

# What is safe sex?

**S**ex is pleasurable, but it's important to be aware of the risks involved and to take precautions. Safe sex is avoiding pregnancy and sexually transmitted infections or diseases, also called STIs, or STDs. Don't rely on someone else to keep you safe and healthy. It's your responsibility. Remember that you can always ask your doctor, a family planning clinic or a sexual health clinic for confidential advice.

## Contraception

If a sperm fertilizes an egg, the woman becomes pregnant. This can happen at any time during a woman's monthly cycle, whether or not her periods are regular. It is the responsibility of both partners to make sure that they are using contraception – protection against pregnancy – unless they want to have a baby together. There are many types of contraception available, some from the chemist and some from the doctor or a family planning centre.

The most commonly used methods are barrier methods, such as condoms, which prevent semen reaching the egg.

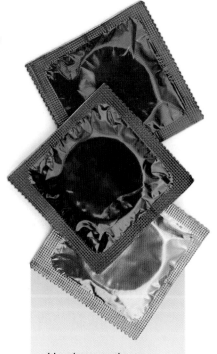

*Condoms*
Thin latex tubes called condoms slip over the penis and prevent semen from spilling out. A female condom fits inside the vagina and prevents sperm reaching the egg. A condom can only be used once. It's important to check the condom has not split during sex.

*Creams*
There are creams called spermicides that kill sperm. They are often used with barrier methods, but they do not prevent pregnancy on their own.

*Used correctly, condoms can help protect against an unwanted pregnancy.*

*Contraceptive pill*
Available from a doctor or family planning clinic, this form of contraception is taken orally by the woman. It alters her hormones to prevent her eggs being fertilized.

## Pregnancy

You can get pregnant when you have a period. You can get pregnant if you have sex standing up. You can get pregnant the very first time you have sex. Sex without proper contraception can lead to pregnancy, wherever and whenever and however the sex takes place.

To be pregnant, not in a relationship, still at school, and with parents who don't know you've started having sex, can be a lonely situation. Unfortunately, it's one which many young people face. Some people decide to end the pregnancy with an abortion. This is an operation in which the foetus (developing baby) is removed from the uterus. Many people are against abortion because it destroys a growing life. Many others believe that it is a woman's right to choose whether or not to continue with a pregnancy.

To avoid such a situation always use effective contraception. However, the only completely sure way to avoid pregnancy is not to have sexual intercourse – contraception methods sometimes fail, especially if they are not used correctly. Remember, no form of contraception is 100% effective.

*Having a baby is a huge, life-changing responsibility.*

# FACTS

✳ In England in 2005, there were 7 pregnancies per 1,000 girls between the ages of 13 and 15. About half of these resulted in abortions.

✳ The United Kingdom has the highest teenage birth rate and abortion rate in western Europe. One report has identified a lack of education about sex and relationships as a factor in this high rate. However, in 2008 the British government made it compulsory to include lessons on relationships and sex for all children aged 5–16.

# In the media

Currently in the United Kingdom, an estimated 10% of school girls will have caught the HPV virus (human papillomavirus) by the time they are 16. This STI is a major cause of cervical cancer, a disease which causes 1,000 deaths a year in the United Kingdom alone. Girls aged 12 and 13 are now offered a vaccination against this virus. The British government believes that this will save many women from developing cervical cancer. However, some people believe that offering the vaccination will only encourage young girls to 'sleep around', and that it would be better to teach them about the dangers of underage sex and STIs.

In 2006, 77% of diagnoses of the chlamydia infection in women occurred in the under 25s. 36% of diagnoses were in 16–19-year-old young women.

## What are STIs?

Safe sex is also about protecting yourself against sexually transmitted infections (STIs). You can catch an STI from any sexual partner who has had sex with someone else who has an STI. STIs are spread in fluids such as semen, vaginal discharge and blood. Wearing a condom helps prevent the spread of STIs.

There are more than 20 STIs. The most common include:

**Chlamydia:** a virus that can affect both men and women. If it is not treated, it can make it more difficult for a woman to become pregnant. There are often no signs that a person has chlamydia.

There are many clinics where young people can get advice and support about practising safe sex.

**HIV:** a virus spread through blood and semen. It can't be caught from touching or kissing, or from toilet seats. HIV can lead to AIDS, which is fatal.

**Genital herpes:** a virus that causes sores around the genitals. Herpes can be treated with antibiotics.

## Keep safe

Signs of an STI include sores, itchiness, redness, pain during sex or when peeing, and discomfort around sex parts. If you suspect you have an infection, see a nurse or doctor or go to a sexual health clinic. Their advice is free and confidential, even if you are under the age of consent. The people in these organizations are there to help you, not to judge. It is a good idea for someone who is sexually active to have regular check-ups because it's not always obvious if a person has an STI.

Anyone who has an STI should not have unprotected sex. They must also tell any sexual partners, so they too can have a check-up and avoid sex until the STI has cleared up. Some STIs can be cleared up with a course of drugs. Others, such as HIV, remain in the body but can be prevented from spreading by using a condom.

Wearing a condom is the best way to avoid catching an STI. It's not a sign of being fussy or uncool – it's safer sex. However, the only way you can be sure of not catching an STI is to avoid sexual contact.

# TALK ABOUT

✳ How do you think discussing and learning about sex and relationships can help young people to develop healthy sexual relationships?

✳ What do you think a healthy sexual relationship means?

# Chapter 6

# What emotions do you feel during puberty?

**P**uberty isn't just about bodily changes, it's a time of emotional change as well. Hormones are responsible for some moods and feelings. Research also shows that an adolescent's brain undergoes changes which can influence their behaviour and mood. The frontal area of the brain, responsible for risk taking, develops during puberty, and some scientists think this is partly why young people are likely to take more risks than children or adults.

## Looks

Puberty makes people more self-conscious. This is bad timing, when the body is hairier, spottier and seemingly more out of control in the looks department. It can make you feel shy and awkward. In today's society, there is a huge amount of emphasis on looks. Not everyone looks like a model and has huge muscles or smooth skin. In fact, most people going through puberty look fairly similar as their bodies are going through the same changes.

*Many young people have anxieties about their looks. One survey found that one in three people aged 10–15 are worried about their body image.*

# TALK ABOUT

Teenagers are often portrayed in the press, on TV and in films as grumpy and greasy.

✳ Do you think this is a myth or is it an accurate reflection of reality?

✳ Does this negative stereotype help or hinder young people in dealing with the changes of puberty?

It's a cliché to say that personality is more important than looks – but it's true. People rarely like people just for their looks; they like people with personality who they can get on well with.

## Freaky me?

Some people feel a bit alarmed about the changes that puberty brings. They may wonder if anyone else grows hair in the oddest places, or keeps having sexual thoughts. These worries can make you feel lonely, especially if you don't want to share them with anyone else. Read and research – and ask questions – and you'll quickly discover that lots of other people have been through similar dilemmas.

*Teenagers often feel that no one understands them, but it helps to try to see other people's viewpoints, too.*

## Feeling low

You might sometimes feel low, and just want to be alone. Shutting the bedroom door for a bit privacy, or listening to music on your MP3 player is all part of growing up, finding your identity as a young adult and becoming more independent. However, if your mood doesn't lift, or you have thoughts about harming yourself, talk to a school nurse, doctor or teacher you trust. If someone is depressed, he or she may need professional help to deal with it.

*Everybody needs private space, and spending time on your own and listening to music, or just thinking, can help you deal with difficult emotions.*

Although puberty is responsible for lots of things, including the release of mood-changing hormones, it doesn't give you the green light for rude, bad behaviour. The people around you will be much more sensitive to your situation if you are respectful and polite.

# It happened to me

'Mum used to keep asking me questions, trying to find out who my friends were and what was going on at school. I just wanted to be on my own. It was really frustrating because I wasn't considered old enough to do all the things my elder sister was allowed to do. And I certainly didn't want to be treated like a little kid. I didn't really know where I fitted in. I guess I was quite moody and probably not very good company.'

Aysha, aged 13.

## School

As well as having your changing body and mind to deal with, there's school. Homework, exams, study, being mature – the pressure can seem never ending. Worries about your body, your friends or fancying someone can all distract you from school work. On the other hand, focusing on your studies could also distract you from worries about looks and friends! If you are finding things a struggle, talk to a teacher, school counsellor or your parents or carers.

## Who am I?

Growing from a child into a young adult can raise doubts about identity: if I am no longer the child who spends every day playing football or playing with toys, who am I? Where do I belong in the world?

It is not easy to have confidence in your own personality when you might feel shy and awkward and don't really know where you fit in. Be as relaxed as possible and you will find your sense of self. It's important to develop a strong sense of self-esteem, so that you can stand up for what you believe and make your own decisions and choices. Develop the confidence to spend time doing the things you like, rather than the things you think you ought to like, or things that other people tell you to do.

*Some people think that taking risks, such as drinking a lot of alcohol, is a sign of being grown-up, but it's far better to do only what you feel good and confident about.*

# Chapter 7

# Relationships

**Y**our body changes, your feelings change – so it's quite likely your relationships with other people will change, too. This change can put pressure on relationships, but if you can be patient those friendships and relationships will emerge stronger.

## Growing up

As you get older, you may find that younger sisters or brothers who you used to play with suddenly become irritating. They walk into your room without knocking, pick up your diary without asking and tell your mum or dad that you fancy so and so. This can make you really furious. Growing up means that relationships change, but try to remember that this is also hard for the other people in your life who aren't at the same stage of development as you.

## Boys and girls

When you were younger, you probably played with both boys and girls without a care in the world. Suddenly, being with members of the opposite sex doesn't seem quite so simple. People often act in a more self-conscious way when in the presence of someone they fancy.

You might wonder what has happened to your love-struck best friend! You can feel rejected if a good friend suddenly abandons you for a boyfriend or girlfriend. Try not to feel left out – a good friend will return to your friendship once the novelty of a new relationship has worn off.

*Try to stay friends, even if one of you has a boyfriend or girlfriend. A friend will still be there for you if the relationship doesn't work out.*

As you and your friends all become more aware of sex and sexuality, it's still quite possible to enjoy being friends with boys and girls. If others tease you about it and suggest you fancy each other, rise above it – enjoy the friendship.

*Friendships between boys and girls don't have to be sexual – they can just be fun!*

## Friendships

Friends come and go all the time. During puberty you become more independent and your views may change. You might find yourself being a bit irritated by friends, or no longer interested in the same things. Perhaps you fall out over what you enjoy doing, or you might get fed up if your friends seem only to talk about boyfriends or girlfriends. But remember that friends will often have similar anxieties to yours; you can talk to them in a way your parents just wouldn't understand. All relationships take time and effort.

# TALK ABOUT

* **What pressures do you think puberty puts on different kinds of relationship?**

* **Do you think there is pressure to have a boyfriend or girlfriend once you reach puberty?**

## Should I have a relationship?

It's your choice. Your friends may be fancying other people and talking about relationships, but there's nothing wrong with being quite happy without a girlfriend or boyfriend. When you meet someone who you want a different type of relationship with, and who you like in a special way, then it may be time to start dating or going out together.

## Sex, sex, sex

If your friends ask you how far you have gone with a girl or boy, they are asking you how much of a sexual relationship you have. It's none of their business. Enjoying touching someone, or being touched in a sexual way, can make a person want to have sex, but it's important to make a considered decision about first having sex. It's also essential to make sure you stay safe.

# It happened to me

'There was this girl at school I really liked. One of my friends told her how I felt. At first, she just blanked me and her friends sniggered whenever I went past. It was horrible. Then I met her in an after school club. We got talking and went out to the cinema together. She was as shy as me, and thought I had been making fun of her. We've only ever held hands and kissed but I keep thinking about her. Being with her makes me feel really happy. I couldn't care less if my friends tease me about not doing more with her – when we're ready, yes.'

Adil, aged 14.

*Choosing to start a sexual relationship should be just that – a choice. It is not right to feel under pressure to have sex just because your friends are or because your boyfriend or girlfriend wants you to.*

A sexual relationship can be most strong, safe and satisfying when two people enjoy a good friendship as well. Sex is a way of showing intimacy. When you meet someone you really like and fancy, don't rush – there is plenty of time to see if you want to develop the relationship sexually. If the person you like puts you under pressure, you might want to question if he or she really cares about you.

If you are putting someone under pressure to do more than he or she feels comfortable with, don't. It can lead to lots of complications, and it doesn't create a caring, supportive sexual relationship.

# TALK ABOUT

* Why do you think people feel pressure to have a boyfriend or girlfriend?

* Do you think it's possible to have a romantic relationship without having sex?

## Parents

Puberty and parents are often an explosive mix. You are growing up and becoming more independent in mind and body but your parents or carers are still responsible for you. You might not agree on many things, but despite any tensions, you love them and they still love you.

## New responsibilities

Your parents keep telling you to behave responsibly, to help more around the house, organize your own things – all because you are a certain age. But then they demand to know where you are going, who with and when you'll be back, and they tell you what you should eat. It's not an easy transition for either young person or parent – try to understand their perspective, and be prepared to make some compromises. Talk openly, clearly and calmly about things from your point of view – and listen and think about their point of view before responding.

You and your parents or carers may have different ideas about how much independence you should have. Rather than argue, try to find a compromise.

Sometimes adults, and not just parents, assume that you are able to deal with certain situations or feelings. As you get older, people's expectations of you increase. This is natural because maturity brings responsibility and independence. However, you may look like an older teenager, but still feel quite young and want to be looked after and protected. Tell adults how you feel.

It's common to compare what your friends are allowed to do with what you're allowed, or not allowed, to do. Try to remember that each family has different ways of working and different rules. If you behave responsibly within the restrictions you have, your family may gradually allow you more freedom.

# TALK ABOUT

❋ **Do you think parents or carers should treat you like a friend, or should there be clear boundaries between a parent and child?**

## Criticism

Sometimes it can seem as if parents and carers only ever criticize you. From the volume of your music to the mess in your room – nothing is ever right. Try to find a middle ground. Ask your parents what puberty was like for them. They may remember it as a time of confusion and feeling self-conscious; or they may remember it as a time when they started fancying people. It will do no harm for them to be reminded how they felt when they were your age – you might even get some advice, or at least have a laugh with them.

*Parents or carers don't have to be your best friends, but they are there to support and guide you.*

# Chapter 8

# Dealing with the changes

**P**uberty is a normal and natural process. There are challenges and new experiences, and probably some ups and downs, but the changing times also allow you to enjoy new things.

## Risks and responsibilities

You may be encouraged to take more risks, such as drinking alcohol and taking drugs. Think situations through. Take your time and don't just follow the crowd. Growing up is about becoming an independent person, not following what your friends say and do.

With age comes responsibility. Don't blow it by going wild, because the chances are the responsibility, freedom and newfound independence will be snatched back from you. Show your parents or carers that you can be trusted and can think through tricky situations.

*Before you act, try to think through the possible consequences of your behaviour.*

## Under pressure

Doubts about yourself can make young people vulnerable to outside suggestions and influences. Not all of these will be good. Sometimes, so-called friends will pressurize you to do things you feel uncomfortable about, or which you disagree with. As you get older, you are more likely to come into contact with people who use illegal drugs, smoke,

drink alcohol and skip school. You may have been involved in these things yourself. Sometimes people do these things to appear more grown-up or cool, or because they are confused and lacking confidence. The bravest thing to do, and often the hardest, is to stand up for what you know is right. If it doesn't feel right or safe, say no and walk away.

Always respect someone's decision to say no to any activity. Whether it's drinking alcohol or being touched sexually, never be afraid to say no. If you feel under pressure in any situation, talk to an adult you trust.

*Feeling good about yourself and believing in yourself will help you to resist being pressurized into doing things that might be bad for you, such as smoking.*

# It happened to me

'I hung around with a group of friends. We'd known each other for ages, but then some of them started drinking a lot – just to get drunk. I couldn't see the point – I liked a bit of drink, but only to feel a bit relaxed. When I said I thought they were being out of order, they laughed at me and said I was pathetic. It really hurt my feelings and I felt so let down by them. But the choice was acting like a prat like them, or doing my own thing and feeling happy.'

Sadie, aged 13.

## Marking puberty

Puberty is a rite of passage. You start as a child and emerge as a young adult. Some cultures and religions celebrate and mark this transition with a coming of age ceremony. This happens at different ages. Some people celebrate with a party when they are 16 or 18, when they are legally allowed to do certain things in their society, such as vote or buy an alcoholic drink. Others celebrate when a girl first has her period.

Puberty is a time to discover new interests and experiences. Once you have reassured yourself that all the physical changes are quite normal, and that you're not some freak of nature, enjoy the opportunities that puberty brings.

# DOs & DON'Ts

* **Don't be pressurized into doing anything you feel unhappy or unsafe about.**

* **Do think about the consequences of your actions before it is too late.**

* **Don't hang around with people who make you feel you have to prove yourself by joining in things you really don't want to.**

* **Do use contraception when you begin to have sex. Get advice from your doctor or a family planning clinic.**

* **Do find ways to feel good about yourself, such as doing things you love.**

* **Do enjoy being with friends who make you feel good about yourself.**

* **Do talk about your feelings, with your friends and adults that you trust.**

# TALK ABOUT

*Becoming a young adult is an exciting time with lots of opportunities for new experiences.*

✳ How can you make puberty a positive experience?

✳ How do you think people could celebrate puberty?

✳ Can you write a list of 10 things that you think are great about puberty?

# Glossary

**acne** An outbreak of spots.

**adolescence** A period of time that starts with puberty and leads to adulthood.

**adolescent** When a person, usually a teenager, goes through adolescence.

**cell** A tiny unit of living matter in the body.

**contraception** Measures taken to prevent a woman becoming pregnant.

**embryo** A developing baby within the uterus.

**erection** When the penis becomes stiff and larger.

**gene** The chemical instruction in DNA which determines how cells grow and function.

**gland** An organ in the body that releases different substances including hormones.

**heterosexual** To be sexually attracted to the opposite sex.

**homosexual** To be sexually attracted to people of the same sex.

**hormones** Chemicals produced by glands which instruct the body to behave in particular ways.

**masturbation** To touch your own sexual parts for pleasure.

**menopause** The physical changes which signal the end of a woman's ability to have children.

**menstruation** The monthly shedding of the uterus lining when a woman is not pregnant.

**oestrogen** The hormone which regulates female sexual characteristics.

**ovaries** Two organs in a woman's body which produce eggs.

**progesterone** The hormone which stimulates the thickening of the walls of the uterus.

**puberty** The period of changing from a child to an adult.

**pubes** An area below the abdomen and around the external sex organs.

**reproductive organs** The sex organs.

**sebaceous gland** A gland in the skin that releases a substance called sebum.

**sexuality** A person's sexual preference. People may be homosexual, heterosexual or bisexual (attracted to both sexes).

**STI** A sexually transmitted infection (also known as an STD).

**stereotype** A fixed idea or view of a group, not taking into account individuality.

**testicles** Two organs in a man's body where sperm is produced.

**testosterone** The hormone which regulates male sexual characteristics.

**vaccination** An injection to give immunity against a disease.

**virus** A germ that causes disease.

# Further information

**Notes for Teachers:**

The Talk About panels are to be used to encourage debate and avoid the polarization of views. One way of doing this is to use 'continuum lines'. Think of a range of statements or opinions about the topics that can then be considered by the pupils. An imaginary line is constructed that pupils can stand along to show what they feel in response to each statement (please see above). If they strongly agree or disagree with the viewpoint they can stand by the signs, if the response is somewhere in between they stand along the line in the relevant place. If the response is 'neither agree, nor disagree' or they 'don't know' then they stand at an equal distance from each sign, in the middle. Alternatively, continuum lines can be drawn out on paper and pupils can mark a cross on the line to reflect their views.

## Books to read

*Puberty* (*Being Healthy, Feeling Great*) by Leon Gray (Wayland, 2009)

*Relationships* (*Being Healthy, Feeling Great*) by Robyn Hardyman (Wayland, 2009)

*Me, Myself and I* by Louise Spilsbury and Mike Gordon (Wayland, 2009)

*Puberty and Your Body* (*Healthy Body*) by Alison Cooper (Wayland, 2007)

*Personal Hygiene* (*Keeping Healthy*) by Carol Ballard (Wayland, 2007)

*Relationships* (*Keeping Healthy*) by Carol Ballard (Wayland, 2007)

## Websites and helplines

**The likeitis website**

Website for boys and girls, with lots of information about teenage issues including puberty.
Website: www.likeitis.org

**The Facts of Life website**

Questions and answers about puberty and growing up, with a parents' and teachers' zone, too.
Website: www.factsoflife.org.uk

**The r u thinking website**

A frank and funky website with lots of questions and answers about sex and relationships.
Website: www.ruthinking.co.uk
Phone: 00 44 (0) 0800 282930
(Free helpline)

**The Family Planning Association**

The Family Planning Association is the United Kingdom's leading sexual health charity.
Website: www.fpa.org.uk
Phone: 00 44 (0) 0845 122 8690
(Free helpline)

**The Child and Youth Health website**

An informative website with lots of information for children and teenagers.
Website: www.cyh.com

**The Kids' Health website**

This website has plenty of information about issues for adolescents.
Website: http://kidshealth.org

**ChildLine**

This website has advice on puberty and sexual feelings.
Website: www.childline.org.uk
Phone: 00 44 (0) 0800 1111
(Free 24-hour helpline)

# Index

Entries in **bold** are for pictures.

# TALK ABOUT

## Contents of titles in the series:

WAYLAND

### Bullying

978 0 7502 4617 0
1. Let's talk about bullying
2. What is bullying?
3. How does it feel to be bullied?
4. Who gets bullied?
5. Why do people bully?
6. Beating bullying
7. Bullying in society

### Eating Disorders and Body Image

978 0 7502 4936 2
1. What are eating disorders?
2. Food and the body
3. What does it mean to have an eating disorder?
4. Who gets eating disorders?
5. What causes eating disorders?
6. Preventing problems
7. The treatment of eating disorders

### Gangs and Knife Crime

978 0 7502 5735 0
1. What are gang and knife crime?
2. Different kinds of gang
3. What do gangs do?
4. Why do people get involved in gangs and knife crime?
5. The effects of gang and knife crime
6. What does the law say?
7. Can we stop gangs and knife crime?
8. Staying safe

### Internet Crime

978 0 7502 5736 7
1. What is Internet crime?
2. Spying, stealing and vandalizing
3. Illegal material on the Internet
4. How chatting online can become a crime
5. Is bullying on the Internet a crime?
6. Music, films and games
7. What can we do to stop Internet crime?

### Sex and Puberty

978 0 7502 5738 1
1. What is puberty? ·
2. What happens to girls during puberty?
3. What happens to boys during puberty?
4. What are sexual feelings?
5. What is safe sex?
6. What emotions do you feel during puberty?
7. Relationships
8. Dealing with the changes

### Drugs

978 0 7502 4937 9
1. What are drugs?
2. Why do we take drugs?
3. What about drinking and smoking?
4. What's the law on drugs?
5. What about cannabis?
6. What other drugs are there?
7. Paying the price
8. It's your choice

### Family Break-Ups

978 0 7502 4934 8
1. What is family break-up?
2. Why do families break up?
3. How do people feel in a family break-up?
4. What happens when a family breaks up?
5. People's attitudes to family break-up
6. The law and family break-up
7. What challenges does the 'new' family face?
8. Moving on

### Homelessness

978 0 7502 5737 4
1. What is homelessness?
2. Why do people become homeless?
3. Homelessness and children
4. Addiction and homelessness
5. Staying clean and healthy
6. Mental health
7. Working and earning
8. Helping the homeless

### Racism

978 0 7502 4935 5
1. What is racism?
2. Why are people racist?
3. What do racists do?
4. Hidden racism
5. What is religious prejudice?
6. Racism against migrants
7. Nazi racial policies
8. What can we do about racism?

### Youth Crime

978 0 7502 4938 6
1. What is crime?
2. Crime past and present
3. Why does youth crime happen?
4. Behaving badly
5. Crimes of theft
6. Crimes of violence
7. What happens if you commit a crime?
8. What can you do about crime?